World Black History

The Struggle *for* Freedom

Spring Hermann

Heinemann Library
Chicago, Illinois

| H | **www.heinemannraintree.com** Visit our website to find out more information about Heinemann-Raintree books. | **To order:** ☏ Phone 888-454-2279 ⌨ Visit www.heinemannraintree.com to browse our catalog and order online. |

©2010 Heinemann Library
an imprint of Capstone Global Library, LLC
Chicago, Illinois

Edited by David Andrews, Louise Galpine, and Abby Colich
Designed by Ryan Frieson and Betsy Wernert
Illustrated by Mapping Specialists
Picture research by Mica Brancic
Originated by Heinemann Library
Printed in China by China Translation & Printing Services Ltd.

13 12 11 10 09
10 9 8 7 6 5 4 3 2 1

Library of Congress Cataloging-in-Publication Data
Hermann, Spring.
  The struggle for freedom / Spring Hermann. -- 1st ed.
    p. cm. -- (World Black history)
  Includes bibliographical references and index.
  ISBN 978-1-4329-2385-3 (hc) -- ISBN 978-1-4329-2392-1 (pb) 1. Slavery--History--Juvenile literature. 2. Slaves--Emancipation--History--Juvenile literature. 3. Antislavery movements--Juvenile literture. 4. Blacks--History--Juvenile literature. I. Title.
  HT861.H47 2009
  306.3'6209--dc22
                        2009003233

Acknowledgments

The author and publishers are grateful to the following for permission to reproduce copyright material: ©Alamy **pp. 8** (The Print Collector), **12, 16** (North Wind Picture Archives), **25** (The London Art Archive); ©The Bridgeman Art Library **pp. 14** (Yale Center for British Art), **15** (Michael Graham-Stewart), **22** (Wilberforce House Museum), **28** (Indivision Charmet), **29** (Giraudon/Lauros/Bibliotheque Nationale, Paris, France), **30** (Clive Uptton), **31** (Peter Newark American Pictures/Private Collection), **33** (Giraudon/Lauros/Bibliotheque Nationale, Paris, France); ©Corbis **pp. 9** (Bettmann), **10** (Bettmann), **17** (Bettmann), **20** (Stapleton Collection), **27, 36** (Bettmann), **37, 40, 41** (Bettmann), **43** (Bettmann); ©Getty Images **p. 13** (MPI/Stringer); ©Heritage Image Partnership **pp. 35** (The Print Collector), **38**; ©Library of Congress **p. 19**; ©North Wind Picture Archives **p. 11**; ©Scala, Florence **pp. 4** (HIP Digital Image 2008), **5**, (HIP Digital Image 2008), **6** (HIP Digital Image 2005), **7** (HIP Digital Image 2008), **21** (HIP Digital Image 2008), **23** (HIP Digital Image 2008), **34** (© ARS, NY and DACS, London 2009 Digital image 2008 © Smithsonian American Art Museum, Washington, DC/Art Resource, New York).

Cover photograph of "On to Liberty" (oil on canvas, 1867), by Theodor Kaufmann (1814-1896) reproduced with permission of the Bridgeman Art Library (©Christie's Images/Private Collection).

We would like to thank Marika Sherwood and Stephanie Davenport for their invaluable help in the preparation of this book.

Contents

Some words are shown in bold, **like this**. You can find out what they mean by looking in the Glossary.

Freedom Lost

In the 1700s, people with African roots lived in all corners of the globe. Meanwhile, their homeland in Africa was as lively and diverse as ever. Native groups and cultures thrived throughout the continent. Trade with European nations spread in the West, but this caused more problems for Africans than it solved. As Europeans began to develop **colonies** in North and South America, they came to Africa to take their most precious resource—the continent's people. The slave trade was tearing African communities apart.

These slaves were marched from Ethiopia across Africa during the slave trade in the 1800s.

The Slave Trade

During the slave trade, more than 60,000 Africans were taken as slaves every year. Some were captured by enemies in war and traded for weapons and other goods. Slave traders also captured Africans, and made their living selling them into slavery. Husbands, wives, and children were separated. Captives were taken away from a land they would never see again. They endured a dangerous trip across the Atlantic Ocean, crammed in a filthy ship. Many got sick or died during the crossing. Others were beaten and abused. Those who lived through the voyage landed on islands in the Caribbean Sea or the coasts of South and North America. White **plantation** owners bought them off an auction block as if they were cattle.

After enslaved Africans were brought across the Atlantic, they were sold on an auction block.

Once Africans were sold to a white owner overseas, slaves were forced to live in a foreign land for the rest of their lives. They lost all freedoms. These men and women had been independent farmers, hunters, craftsmen, healers, and elders. Now they were the property of their owner, with no rights. A slave's only role was now to serve his or her master. A slave's skills now belonged to his or her owner. Whites did not believe that they were wrong or evil to own Africans. They convinced themselves that their black slaves were not equal to white people, and that they therefore could be owned.

From the mid-1700s to the late-1800s, enslaved Africans struggled for their freedom. A few lost hope. Some protested. Many joined in revolts and rebelled against their slavery. And by the end of the 1800s, almost all slaves throughout Africa, Europe, and North and South America would be free.

The Hard Life of a Slave

Most enslaved Africans were sold to owners of **plantations**. Plantations were large farms that required many workers. The white owners lived in large houses. They used enslaved men, women, and children to run their plantations. Slaves also ran small businesses for their owners. Slaves worked in gristmills to grind corn or wheat and in sawmills to make lumber. George Washington, the first president of the United States, used slaves to run his whiskey **distillery**.

"Breaking In" the Enslaved

When enslaved Africans arrived, many were weak, angry, and scared. Most could not speak European languages. So each new slave was "broken in" by slaves who were already there. The newly enslaved were shown their new work and warned to obey the rules. The master's **overseers** expected slaves to obey. Slaves had to learn a new language by listening to other slaves.

Slaves were forced to do the dangerous job of harvesting sugar cane.

Overseers controlled slaves with whips. Spikes are around this slave's neck to keep him from lying down.

Slave Discipline

Often hundreds of enslaved Africans lived on a plantation with the master and his family. Overseers were hired to control the slaves. The overseer was usually white, but sometimes an experienced slave was appointed as an overseer. An overseer was firm and could be cruel. If a slave did not obey orders, the overseer punished him. A slave might be chained and starved or whipped.

Arthur Greene, a slave from Virginia, recalled how the overseers made slaves go to the woods and cut the sticks used for beatings. Greene said the overseers whipped slaves "until blood ran down like water. Then they wash you down in salt and pepper." This made the wounds sting even worse. Greene saw "whipping machines" that could beat a slave without wearing out the overseer's arm. However, some masters were more humane. They gave rewards, such as a little more food or better jobs, and did not allow severe punishments.

The Sugar Mill.

The Sugar works

The Sugar canes

Plantation Work

To grow crops in North and South America, large gangs of workers called **field hands** were needed. There were no tractors or modern machines to help. Planting and harvesting was done by the backbreaking labor of the slaves.

Sugar Cane and Tobacco

Sugar cane was grown in the tropical climates of Brazil and Caribbean islands such as Jamaica, Barbados, and Cuba. Cane growing was brutal and dangerous work year-round. Sugar came from cutting the leaves off the tall plants, then crushing the cane in a mill and boiling the juice. As the demand for sugar in Europe and America grew, slaves had to work harder to produce it.

Tobacco became very popular in the 1700s. Europeans smoked it in pipes or sniffed it. Planted mainly in the British **colony** of Virginia, tobacco needed great care to grow. Enslaved children, sometimes as young as eight, pulled worms off the tobacco leaves. Older slaves cut the leaves, dried or "cured" them, and produced the tobacco.

Cotton and Rice

Cotton was grown in the British colonies in the West Indies and along the North American coast. New machines were invented in the 1700s to clean cotton, spin thread, and weave cloth. These machines made cotton an even bigger **cash crop**. Slaves picked the cotton **bolls** and removed bugs from the plants. Enslaved men and women bent their backs picking, sometimes until they were crippled.

Rice needed a certain soil and climate to grow, but it made a good profit. Slaves from the African area of present-day Sierra Leone had been rice farmers. Rice farmers in the colonies of South Carolina and Georgia bought these slaves because they would know how to farm rice. Enslaved men planted, then dug ditches to flood the rice. Enslaved females pounded the rice after harvest to prepare it to sell.

Slaves work in a cotton field in the southern United States.

Slaves in British-Ruled Virginia

One of the first **colonies** in North America the British settled was Virginia. Virginia depended on enslaved Africans for its economy. **Plantation** owners purchased slaves at huge auctions. Enslaved men, women, and children were lined up and examined, as if they were animals. They were sold to the highest bidder. Later, slaves could be traded from one master to another.

This newspaper shows an advertisement for an auction in which whites can come purchase black slaves.

A Field Hand's Life

On a plantation, most of the slaves had to plant the fields or care for livestock in barns. These workers were called **field hands**. **Overseers** controlled them. Slaves seldom saw the master. Enslaved families left their cabin at dawn and walked to a distant job site. Former slave Henrietta Petty recalled her grueling job in the 1850s:

> Work from sun[rise] to sun[set] in that old tobacco field. Work til my back felt like it ready to pop in two. Us black people had to look after tobacco like it was gold.... Got a lashing if you cut a leaf before it's ripe.

Slaves sometimes slept crowded together on the ground of a log hut. Instead of blankets and pillows, many used sticks, straw, and old rags. On Saturday night on some plantations, slaves socialized with one another. They sang, danced, or told stories. These parties were the few occasions when slaves could enjoy themselves. These gatherings helped slaves maintain a sense of community and hope that they would survive and one day be free.

A House Servant's Life

Some slaves cared for the master's house and family. These slaves were called **house servants**. These jobs included maids, butlers, cooks, seamstresses, laundresses, and stable hands. These slaves had to labor all day, too, and were on call at night. Caring for their owners' children was a demanding job only given to enslaved females.

Enslaved children started working at about age seven. Thomas Jefferson, who became the third President of the United States, put his slave boys to work by age ten. They did jobs like hammering iron into nails in his nail shop. Enslaved children were not permitted to go to school. Sometimes, however, they still managed to find ways to learn how to read and write.

Religion for Slaves

A slave's Sundays were for family and worship. Many masters let slaves garden, fish, and hunt to supplement their own family's **rations**. House servants often went to church services with their owners. Slaves had to sit in segregated sections of the church and were not allowed to sit with their owners. Many slaves also maintained their own traditions with African songs, dances, and rituals. These practices, passed on through word of mouth, were blended with Christian **hymns** and prayers.

Slaves had no church buildings, but some used a small cabin or the open air. Their preachers were slaves, too. They worked the fields during the week, and on Sundays were permitted to preach what they managed to teach themselves. These preachers gave hope that at least in heaven, slaves would be free and happy with God.

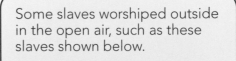

Some slaves worshiped outside in the open air, such as these slaves shown below.

Slaves legally could not get married, but sometimes their masters allowed marriage ceremonies, such as this one shown here. Masters thought that if a slave had a family, he'd be less likely to run away.

Who Was Family?

After they were shipped from Africa during the slave trade, slaves lost the status and role they enjoyed there. The families they had in Africa were nothing but a memory. Enslaved men and women had to create new families on plantations. Slaves were not allowed to marry. But some masters saw that marriage could be useful. Slaves were likely to work harder and not run away if they had family around them.

Slave Marriages

Fannie Berry, a former slave born in 1840, recalled being married in a white woman's parlor. Her female attendants walked her down the aisle to the preacher and she took her groom's hand. After the ceremony (which usually included the African custom of the couple jumping over a broom), Fannie and her husband had a feast and square danced.

Masters wanted their slaves to have children. Some enslaved women were forced to have children with many enslaved men, or with their owners. The children would become slaves too. The masters often felt no connection to the children and would sell them without hesitating.

13

Slavery and the British

By 1600 Britain had also begun participating in the slave trade. Capturing African slaves and selling them to whites in the Caribbean and North America made many British merchants rich. Through the 1600s and 1700s, British slave merchants carried over one-third of all African slaves sold across the Atlantic. By 1780 Britain controlled **colonies** in the areas that are now Newfoundland, Nova Scotia, the United States, Bermuda, the Bahamas, Belize, Jamaica, and the Lesser Antilles islands. Many of these colonies used African slaves.

Africans Come to Britain

Merchants and **plantation** owners in the Americas often also had mansions in Britain, where they used personal slaves. African slaves and **discharged** African sailors arrived in London, Liverpool, and other port cities. Some Africans came to London as enslaved children. Women of the 1700s liked to be served by African children dressed up in fancy costumes.

These masters in Britain are being served by an enslaved child.

In the late 1700s, more African men settled in ports around Britain. In exchange for freedom, these men had fought for Britain in the Seven Years' War (1756–1763) or the American Revolution (1775–1783). With the colonies lost, the British economy was slumping, and jobs were hard to find. London's free Black Britons worked as porters, street vendors, and taxi-men. Women worked in people's homes. Some begged or worked in taverns.

Ignatius Sancho

Ignatius Sancho was an enslaved African child owned by three sisters. As a young man, he met a nobleman, the Duke of Montagu, who helped educate Sancho. Later, Sancho escaped and went looking for the duke. He discovered that the duke had died, but the duke's wife decided to hire Sancho as a butler.

Sancho had many interests, including writing, music, and acting. With money he saved, he opened a grocery store in London. But he is most remembered for his writing. His wonderful letters were the first published protest against slavery written by an African.

Resisting Slavery

More than anything, those who were enslaved longed for liberty. **Overseers** or masters might hear slaves talking about wanting to be free and inflict punishment. So slaves kept quiet about this longing. However, many slaves showed their dissatisfaction in other ways.

Silent Protests

Worker slow-downs were one way to fool the master. This meant doing a job much more slowly than necessary. It was risky to do this unless slaves were in a group. A master or overseer might notice if only one slave was slowing down.

Faking sickness or injury was another way to protest. However, many masters made slaves work even when sick. Other slaves pretended they did not know how to do the job assigned to them. Slaves became clever at acting "stupid." It allowed a slave to work slowly and get more rest time. "Losing" or breaking tools was another form of protest.

These slaves are attempting to escape to the North during the United States Civil War.

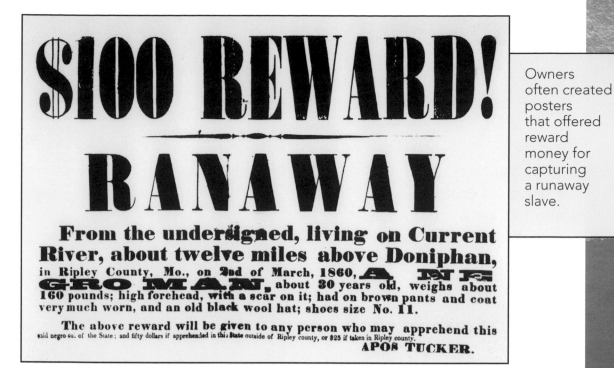

$100 REWARD!

RANAWAY

From the undersigned, living on Current River, about twelve miles above Doniphan, in Ripley County, Mo., on 2nd of March, 1860, A NEGRO MAN, about 30 years old, weighs about 160 pounds; high forehead, with a scar on it; had on brown pants and coat very much worn, and an old black wool hat; shoes size No. 11.

The above reward will be given to any person who may apprehend this said negro out of the State; and fifty dollars if apprehended in this State outside of Ripley county, or $25 if taken in Ripley county.

APOS TUCKER.

Owners often created posters that offered reward money for capturing a runaway slave.

Hiding or Escaping

Sometimes slaves would manage to escape to the woods and hide with the support of fellow slaves. This allowed slaves to escape from the cruel treatment of overseers. But eventually, hidden slaves were likely to be caught, and their helpers punished.

Slaves on Caribbean islands had few places to hide. But in the United States, there were many places for escaped slaves to go. Masters hired **slave patrollers** and slave hunters to catch their runaway slaves. They also advertised rewards in the newspapers for capturing runaways. A slave was valuable property. So masters searched for their slaves, sometimes for years after they had run away.

Buying Freedom

Some slaves purchased their freedom. This was possible only with more humane owners. Sometimes a slave with important skills was leased to neighbors, who then paid the slave's owner. If a slave's owner let the slave keep a small part of this payment, the slave might one day save up enough to buy his or her freedom.

Difficulty Escaping

Overseers, vigilant owners, slave patrollers, hunting dogs, and bounty hunters kept slaves in bondage. A runaway might get lost in the woods or starve to death. If caught, a slave's punishment was brutal. Many slaves were too old or sickly to make the run. If a slave reached the North where slavery was illegal, he or she might never see relatives, children, or friends again.

Ona Judge's Escape

Ona (pronounced "Oney") Judge was a young, talented seamstress. Her father was a white servant. Her mother Betty was a slave of Martha Washington, wife of president George Washington. When he became the president of the United States, Ona was taken to the Capital in Philadelphia to serve Martha Washington. There she met free **African Americans**. She longed to live a free life as they did. Still a teenager, Ona escaped to New Hampshire in 1796 and hid. Washington tried to have her captured and returned. After the Washingtons died, Ona married and had three children. She was often poor. When asked if she missed the comforts the "first family" of the United States had provided her, she replied, "No, I am free."

Black Population, enslaved and free, in 1790

STATE/TERRITORY	FREE	ENSLAVED
Connecticut	2,771 (51%)	2,648
Delaware	3,899 (30%)	8,887
Georgia	398 (1.3%)	29,264
Kentucky	114 (1%)	12,430
Maine	536 (100%)	---
Maryland	8,043 (7%)	103,063
Massachusetts	5,369 (100%)	---
New Hampshire	630 (80%)	157
New Jersey	2,762 (19%)	11,423
New York	4,682 (18%)	21,193
North Carolina	5,041 (5%)	100,783
Pennsylvania	6,531 (64%)	3,707
Rhode Island	3,484 (78%)	958
South Carolina	1,801 (2%)	107,094
Tennessee	361 (10%)	3,417
Vermont	269 (100%)	---
Virginia	12,866 (4%)	292,627

The Escapes of Moses Bell

Moses Bell was a slave and a work foreman. His master was John Fallons of Virginia. According to Bell's nephew Frank, Moses' master and other slaves respected Moses. Yet Moses wanted true freedom. Frank said that "every year when **Indian summer** come [through the 1850s], … [Moses] would run away." John Fallons sent slave catchers to capture Moses before he made it to the northern states, where slavery was illegal. It was expensive to track a slave, and Moses escaped ten times. Frank said that "finally old Master got plumb tired of looking all over Alexandria for Uncle Moses." The next time Moses was recaptured, Fallons sold him to owners in the South. The only freedom Moses Bell ever experienced was during those ten times he ran away.

Slaves, pictured here in 1864, knew they would never see their families or friends again if they tried to escape.

Opposition to Slavery Grows

After the American **colonies** won their freedom from Britain, the new nation's founders wrote a Constitution in 1789. This Constitution let each state decide whether or not it would allow slavery.

Southern states allowed slavery to continue. Northern states such as Massachusetts, New York, Connecticut, Rhode Island, and New Jersey did not. As a result, angry feelings between the North and the South began to grow.

Thomas Clarkson and William Wilberforce

Two of the greatest advocates for ending the slave trade were Englishmen Thomas Clarkson and William Wilberforce. Clarkson interviewed black former seamen he found in British ports. They told him of the hardships of slavery. Clarkson, along with fellow activist Granville Sharp, created the Committee for the Abolition of the Slave Trade.

William Wilberforce, a member of the British Parliament, read Clarkson's writings against slavery. He decided to sponsor the cause of abolition in Parliament. But slave trading was a big business. It took many years before slave merchants would give it up. Thanks to abolitionists, the slave trade was outlawed in 1807.

William Wilberforce

Quakers, shown here in a meeting in 1640, were the first group to call for the end of slavery everywhere.

Antislavery Groups Form

Early **Quaker** groups in Britain and its colonies believed that slavery was against the word of God. They wanted it outlawed. Other Christians believed slavery was not condemned by the Bible. They did not want slavery to end.

The first society in America to call for the abolition of slavery was formed by the American Quakers of Pennsylvania in 1775. Their goal was to end slavery everywhere. Antislavery societies expanded until there was one in each of the northern states. Protests against slavery in Britain began in the 1700s. Out of the estimated 14,000 Black Britons, very few were enslaved. Most were free, or **bound servants**. But in the British colonies, **plantation** owners held many slaves.

France Releases Its Slaves

France was the first European nation to outlaw slavery in its colonies. Jacques Pierre Brissot organized the Society of the Friends of the Blacks in 1788. The Constitution of France, passed in 1795, **abolished** slavery. But when Napoleon Bonaparte became dictator four years later, he allowed slavery to return.

Arguing Against Slavery

Many of those who spoke loudest against slavery were slaves themselves. Some, such as former slaves Ottobah Cugoano and Olaudah Equiano, wrote books about their experiences. These books showed the evils of slavery.

An American slave named James Somerset was brought to London in 1772 by his master. His master planned to sell Somerset to a Caribbean plantation, but Somerset escaped. Antislavery activists protected him and helped him plead for his freedom in court. Amazingly, the judge, Lord Mansfield, ruled in favor of Somerset. He said: "I cannot say this case is approved by the law of England… therefore the black must be **discharged**."

Posters such as this one called for the end of slavery.

The End of the Slave Trade

The **transatlantic slave trade** was finally outlawed by Britain in 1807. In the United States, the Constitution said that after 1808 "importation of persons" should stop. However, the trade continued illegally. From 1808 to 1860, British and American navies seized 1,600 illegal slave ships and freed 150,000 captured Africans. Millions more slaves were taken from Africa without eventually being released.

Olaudah Equiano

As an Ibo child (in what is now Nigeria), Olaudah Equiano was kidnapped from his home when his parents were away and sold into slavery. He was bought and sold several times and given several new names. One master was a naval captain who took him to many places around the world.

Under another owner, Equiano was able to earn money to buy his freedom in 1766. He worked in the trade business in the West Indies and London. In 1773 he joined an expedition to search for the Northwest Passage, a route through the Arctic to the Pacific Ocean.

Equiano later moved to London and became a leading figure in the abolition campaign. The story he wrote of his life, *The Interesting Narrative of the Life of Olaudah Equiano the African*, became very popular in 1789 and sold out nine editions during his life.

The Back to Africa Movement

More white people began to agree that slavery should end. But many did not want thousands of independent blacks to settle in Britain or the United States. They were concerned that black people would take the jobs and land they wanted. They searched for a way to get them sent somewhere else.

The British Freetown Plan

In 1787 the British abolitionists purchased land on the West African coast (now Sierra Leone) and established Freetown. They settled over 2,000 blacks there, including those who sided with them in the American Revolution. More were sent over, and Africans freed from slave ships joined them. These liberated Africans tried to rule the area, but the British had trading forts in Sierra Leone, Gold Coast (now Ghana), and Gambia. The native peoples, such as the **Mende**, were angry with the British for taking over their land. Native people did not believe that land could be "sold." They attacked the British traders and the resettled Africans. However, new settlers kept coming.

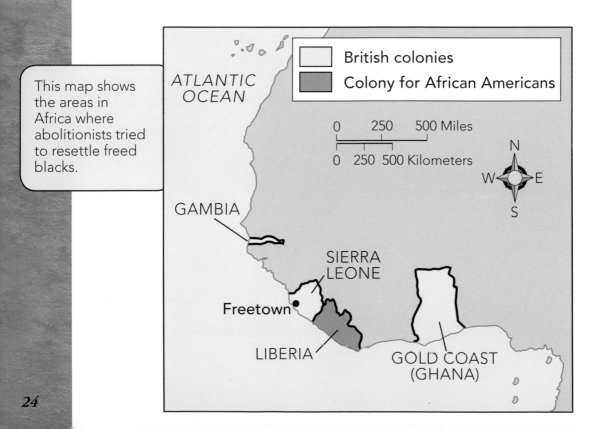

This map shows the areas in Africa where abolitionists tried to resettle freed blacks.

British colonies
Colony for African Americans

0   250   500 Miles

0   250 500 Kilometers

N
W E
S

ATLANTIC OCEAN

GAMBIA

SIERRA LEONE

Freetown

LIBERIA

GOLD COAST (GHANA)

This image shows the settlement of Freetown along the coast of present-day Sierra Leone.

The American Colonization Society

In 1817 the American Colonization Society (ACS) was created to help set Africans free and transport them to another location. Most leaders in the colonization movement were white clergymen or slave owners. Some were free blacks. Paul Cuffe, born in Massachusetts, to an African father and a Native American mother, also wanted to resettle freed slaves. A former slave himself, Cuffe became rich as a trader and ship owner. In 1815 he shipped 38 black settlers and supplies to Sierra Leone at his own expense. He died in 1817 before he could complete his plan.

In 1819 the United States Congress granted $100,000 for ACS agents to "buy" land in Africa and return slaves illegally taken out of that continent. Many slave owners wanted to be paid to free their slaves, but there was no money to pay them for this. Therefore, most slaves were not freed. Many Africans who were free wished to remain in the United States, the only home they knew.

Settling in Liberia

The country of Liberia is located on the west coast of Africa. It lies south of Sierra Leone and north of the Ivory Coast. Liberia was not claimed by a European nation as a colony during the **Scramble for Africa**. So Americans thought of it as free. Yet it was the homeland of many native peoples. The Vai, the Gola, the Loma, the Dei, the Bassa, and others lived throughout the territory.

The Right to Sell Land

United States presidents James Madison and James Monroe (both slave masters) supported sending freed **African Americans** to an African colony. In 1820 President Monroe sent agents to buy tracts of land in Liberia from some native kings. But other native groups did not recognize these land "sales." Confusion and anger between groups resulted. None of them wanted the freed slaves to take over their territory in Liberia.

The United States set up a government center. They named this city Monrovia after President Monroe. Thousands of settlers arrived and were given farms. Military forces arrived to protect the settlers. The natives wanted the new residents to leave. Conflicts exploded among the new settlers, the American forces, and the native groups who felt the land was theirs. Some native leaders were furious at other kings for "selling" the land and declared war on them.

Return to Africa

The American Colonization Society sent its first group of settlers to Sherbro Island, off the coast of Sierra Leone, in 1820. However, many settlers died of disease in the swampy island. In 1821 representatives set out to find better land along the coast.

At Cape Mesurado, they persuaded the local peoples—some say by force—to sell an area that was 59 kilometers (36 miles) long and 5 kilometers (3 miles) wide. In return, they were offered weapons, rum, and other supplies. The survivors from Sherbro Island moved to Cape Mesurado in 1822 to build their settlement.

Liberia Gains Independence

In 1847 the Republic of Liberia became independent of the United States. But battles between the settlers and the native tribal leaders went on through the 1800s. The plan to make Liberia a new home for African Americans was a failure. Native peoples kept resisting.

In the United States, African Americans faced extreme prejudice. They had limited chances for education and jobs. But most African Americans believed they were better off in the United States. It was their country, and they wanted to stay.

The United States created settlements in Liberia for freed slaves.

Slave Rebellions

White masters greatly feared slave rebellions. They kept their slaves under tight control. Slaves had few chances to make weapons. Organizing rebellions was not easy. Yet many slaves fought to free their brothers and sisters in bondage. Here are the stories of slaves who led rebellions in the Caribbean.

Haiti Struggles for Freedom

Toussaint Louverture was born a slave on a sugar **plantation** in 1743, in what is now Haiti. He received some education. Freed at age 33, he became a rebel commander. He helped plan a rebellion against the French rulers in 1791. Six years later, Louverture ousted the French and freed the slaves. Governor from 1797 until 1802, his government traded actively with the United States. But Louverture was sent to prison by Napoleon in 1802. He told the French: "In overthrowing me, you have cut down...only the trunk of the tree of liberty. It will spring up again by the roots." After his death in 1803, Louverture's army rallied. His former generals won freedom for all in Haiti.

Toussaint Louverture led rebellions, eventually helping free slaves in Haiti.

Many slaves revolted in the Caribbean in the 1800s

Barbados Revolts

An African slave named Bussa began a revolt on the sugar plantations of Barbados in 1816. Slaves set fire to the cane fields, causing massive destruction. Although the Barbadian slaves did not kill their owners, hundreds of them were executed after the failure of the rebellion.

Jamaican Slaves Revolt

Sam Sharpe, a slave in Montego Bay, Jamaica, was an educated man and a Baptist preacher. Sam asked his fellow slaves to protest with "**passive resistance**." They would refuse to work on Christmas Day of 1831. Then they would insist on better treatment. White masters heard of this and turned the war ships' guns on Montego Bay. Violence broke out. Sharpe led a revolt that lasted eight days. Fourteen whites died and more than 300 slaves were executed for rebelling. Sam Sharpe was hanged in 1832. Most agree that slave revolts like Sam Sharpe's eventually led the British to **abolish** slavery in 1833.

Slaves Rebel in the United States

Rebellion in the United States was just as dangerous as it was in Jamaica. Most rebels were captured and killed. There are many stories of enslaved and free blacks who risked everything for a chance at freedom.

The Unlucky Lottery Winner

Denmark Vesey was born in West Africa. After serving as a sea captain for 20 years, Denmark Vesey won a lottery. He used the prize money to buy his freedom and start a carpenter shop in the United States. Vesey wanted all **African Americans** to rise up and fight. Over 9,000 enslaved and free blacks joined his revolt in 1822. They were ready to raid an **arsenal** of weapons and take over Charleston, South Carolina.

Rumors about the plot reached the city's whites. Vesey and his leaders were captured right before the planned raid. When he and 46 others were hanged, the rebellion ended.

Slaves in the southern United States led revolts they hoped would one day lead to freedom.

The Rebel Blacksmith

Gabriel, slave of Thomas Prosser in Richmond, Virginia, was a skilled blacksmith. He often was permitted to work in town. Smart and organized, Gabriel managed to communicate with many other slaves. He planned his slave revolt in 1800. With recruits from three cities, he would take over Richmond, capital of Virginia, and capture its armory. His plan, however, was betrayed just as it began. A slave owner was told about the plan, and a state militia was brought in to stop the rebellion. Gabriel and his men were finally captured. The leaders were hanged.

A Man of Destiny

Nat Turner, a slave of the Turner family in northern Virginia, was very religious and thought it was his destiny to free the slaves. He said God sent him a vision to form an army. In 1831 Nat and his army killed at least 55 whites in their rampage for freedom. Although Nat and his leaders were caught and executed, whites did not stop there. They were determined to terrify slaves into submission. They murdered any slave who caused the least bit of trouble. Masters displayed the heads of the murdered slaves by the roadside.

Nat Turner led a slave revolt before being captured and murdered.

On the Road to Freedom

A slave's best chance at freedom was to get to a land where slavery had been **abolished**. In the southern United States, slaves risked their lives to escape to northern states or Canada, while others headed south for Mexico or the Caribbean. The path they took was called the **Underground Railroad**.

This map shows the various routes of the Underground Railroad, which led many slaves to freedom.

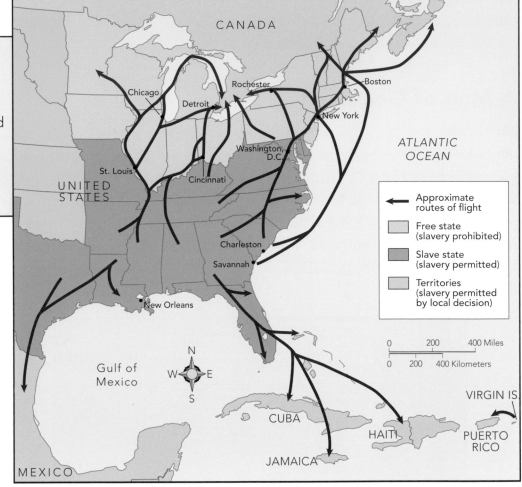

The Underground Railroad was a secret network of over three thousand volunteers. Free **African Americans** and white abolitionists joined together to help escaped slaves reach free states. But even reaching a free state did not end the danger. A law said slave catchers could still recapture escaped slaves and return them to their masters. So volunteers kept moving slaves farther north, using hiding places called "stations" or "depots." Runaways hid in people's cellars or barns, or on boats or trains.

The Underground Railroad in Indiana

Indiana's Antislavery League knew the favorite spots for runaways to cross into their state. Many escaped from Kentucky, where the Wabash River met the Ohio River. From there, volunteers brought the slaves upriver. The "Railroad" took them into Michigan, where another group took them into Canada.

North to Canada

Canada was a perfect place for escaped slaves. Few African slaves had been bought in Canada, and in 1793, Canada outlawed the slave trade. So the Underground Railroad took people across the northern borders of Michigan, New York, and Vermont to Canada. It was a long, hard trek. Some had to cross a frighteningly high footbridge near Niagara Falls. They resettled in Canadian cities.

William Still

William Still of Philadelphia was born a free African American. He became a successful merchant, and headed the Philadelphia Vigilance Committee. He kept records of the slaves who escaped through his city, and helped hide them. Then he prepared them to escape into the state of New York on the Underground Railroad. His work freed hundreds of slaves.

Many escaped slaves braved climbing a dangerous footbridge along Niagara Falls, shown here, to reach freedom in Canada.

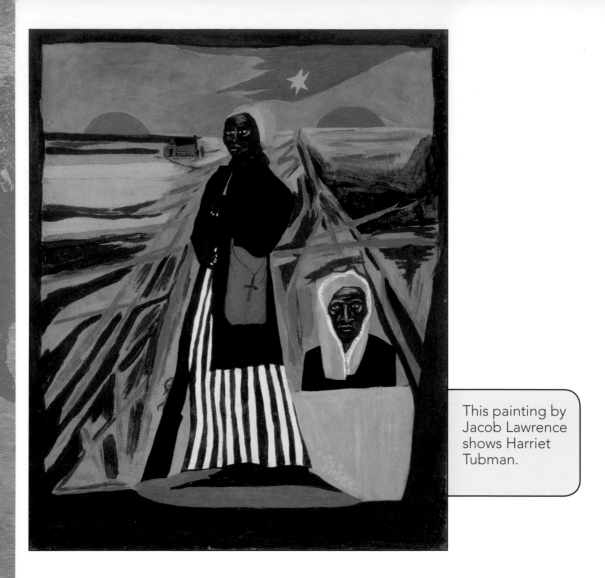

This painting by Jacob Lawrence shows Harriet Tubman.

Guiding Others to Freedom

Harriet Tubman, an enslaved African American, always dreamed of liberty. Her Maryland **plantation** master beat her and said he would sell her into the Deep South if she ran away. Her husband, a free man, would not run with her. So at age 20, Harriet escaped alone.

With only the night stars to guide her, Harriet made it into Pennsylvania. She said she felt like she had arrived in heaven. But she would not have time to enjoy her freedom. When she heard that some members of her family would be sold to a new owner, she returned to Maryland and helped them escape. Still, Harriet wanted to do more. She risked her life 19 more times by sneaking back into Maryland. She ushered hundreds of slaves into free states.

A Difficult Road

The long, dangerous trip north on the Underground Railroad by foot and boat was more than some slaves could handle. They became too frightened and tired. They begged Harriet to let them return to their master. Harriet carried loaded guns. She told these people bluntly that she would shoot them before she let them turn around. If caught, they would be forced to tell where the rest of Harriet's runaways were.

Harriet was tough and strong. She was never caught. She claimed never to have lost a "passenger" on the Railroad. When the United States Civil War broke out, Harriet became a hospital nurse for the Union army. She even spied on Confederate forces who wanted slavery to remain legal.

The freed slaves called Harriet "Moses." Like Moses, the biblical leader who led his people out of Egyptian slavery, Harriet guided her people safely to freedom.

Harriet Tubman helped hundreds of slaves escape to freedom.

Standing Up for Liberty

Many of the enslaved spoke out for themselves in court or in the press. They came from different cultures, but wanted the same thing: freedom and respect.

Frederick Douglass

Born of an enslaved mother and a white father in 1818, Frederick Douglass escaped from slavery in Maryland in 1838. Although a fugitive, he educated himself. Soon he was speaking out against slavery. While in Britain, Douglass found friends who raised money to buy his freedom. At age 28, Douglass went home a free man to start a newspaper, *The North Star*. A powerful abolitionist, he wrote: "Truth is of no color—God is father of us all, and we are all Brethren." In 1872 the liberty party nominated him as the first African American to run for vice president of the United States.

Frederick Douglass was an important figure in the abolitionist movement.

Slaves being sent to Cuba to be sold revolted on their ship, *La Amistad*, in 1839.

La Amistad Revolt

Sengbe Pieh, a **Mende** rice farmer from West Africa, was captured by slave traders in 1839. He was shipped overseas, to be sold in Cuba. He and his fellow captives fought back and took over their ship, *La Amistad*. While trying to sail back to Africa, they were captured and imprisoned in the United States. Pieh became the group's leader. He said: "It is better to die than be a white man's slave." Before the United States Supreme Court, they were judged to be human victims, not property. Abolitionists and missionaries raised money for the thirty-five survivors to return home.

Jamaican Heroes

In the late 1820s in Jamaica, two free Black Britons, Robert Osborn and Edward Jordan, advocated for black rights through the newspaper they produced, *The Watchman*. They wrote about abolition and crusaded for free Black Britons' rights to vote and own property. In 1830 Jordan was charged with treason by the British government. When he was found not guilty, he and Osborn were heroes to their community. Jordan and Osborn kept on writing for the rights of blacks everywhere.

Freedom at Last

By 1830 the idea of **abolishing** slavery was gaining more support. Around the world, governments began to recognize the evils of slavery. However, ending the practice took years.

Britain Outlaws Slavery

The British Parliament voted in 1833 to end slavery throughout most of its **colonies**. All slaves had to be freed by 1838. But during the 1830s, runaway slaves were still treated violently.

British slave masters were given £20 million (about $2 billion today) for releasing their slaves. Each colony made its own decision about how to free their blacks in bondage. Bermuda and Antigua freed their slaves all at once, while Jamaica freed its slaves more gradually. In the British colony of India, many Africans, as well as native Indians, remained enslaved until 1868.

These slaves in the Caribbean celebrate news of their freedom.

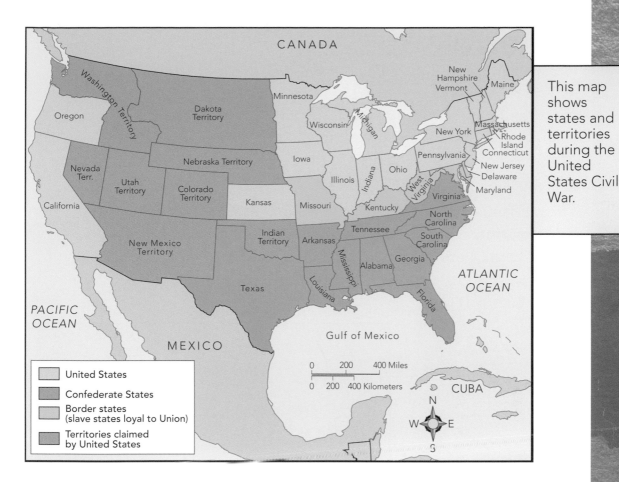

This map shows states and territories during the United States Civil War.

Ending Slavery in the United States

The United States government did not pay slaveowners to release their slaves. Each state had the power to decide whether slavery would remain legal. This situation led to a terrible war.

States in the North outlawed slavery. Many people wanted slavery to be illegal in any new state that formed. But states in the South rebelled and tried to form a new country. They became the Confederate States of America. States on the border between the North and the South (Missouri, Maryland, Delaware, and Kentucky) did allow slavery, but they remained loyal to the United States government (also called the Union).

At first, the American Civil War was fought over the power of the states to make their own laws. It was about differences between the North (which was mostly industrial) and the South (which was mostly agricultural). Gradually, it also became about abolishing slavery. The war began in April 1861 and lasted four bloody years.

Fighting for Freedom

President Abraham Lincoln had reasons not to allow **African American** soldiers in the Union military. He believed soldiers from the border states would refuse to fight beside African Americans, and would join the Confederates. He knew many white soldiers were biased against serving with African American soldiers. Even in the North, many whites were afraid of giving weapons to African Americans.

Then in January 1863, President Lincoln signed the **Emancipation Proclamation**. This document said that all slaves in the United States—including the Confederate states—were free. When the war became about ending slavery, African American soldiers were allowed to join the fight. From 1863 to 1865, about 200,000 African Americans served in the Union Army, and 30,000 sailed with the Union Navy. Almost 40,000 gave their lives in the war.

By signing the Emancipation Proclamation, President Abraham Lincoln declared all slaves in the United States free.

Amending the Constitution

After the Union won the Civil War, three amendments to the Constitution were passed to assure freedoms to all former slaves. Here are the freedoms that they assured:

13th Amendment (1864) Slavery could never exist in the United States.

14th Amendment (1868) All freed slaves were now full citizens.

15th Amendment (1870) No man could be denied the right to vote due to race, color, or previous enslavement.

Hearing the News

It took a long time before the Emancipation Proclamation had an effect in the South. Masters in the South did not free their slaves, and kept the Proclamation quiet. Slaves who couldn't read did not see the news in the newspapers. When they finally discovered they were free, many cried and burst into song, singing, "Slavery chain is broken at last!" For many, it seemed too good to be true. Charles Grandy, an African American cook in the Union Army, said, "The Army had to stay in the South twelve months before they could make the [former slaves] know they was free!"

A Union soldier tells an enslaved family that they are **emancipated**.

Emancipation Spreads

The Civil War did not end slavery around the world. In the years that followed, however, more nations ended the cruel practice.

In 1880 Cuba, still under Spanish control, outlawed slavery. But these freed slaves were required to work for their former owners for eight more years. However, in 1886 the king of Spain set the former slaves free forever.

Controlled by Portugal in 1880, Brazilian abolitionists pushed a bill to end slavery by 1890. **Plantation** owners fought it. However, immigrant labor from Europe flooded Brazil. It was cheaper to pay them than keep slaves. In a bloodless revolt, slavery ended in Brazil in 1888.

Ending Slavery Around the World

Slavery was abolished at different times throughout the world. Here are the dates in which slavery was abolished in a few countries:

1818	Holland
1829	Mexico
1833	Great Britain
1848	France
1865	United States
1873	Puerto Rico
1886	Cuba
1888	Brazil

Freedom in Africa

In parts of Africa, slavery had been a common practice for centuries. However, "slaves" in African cultures were treated much better than those enslaved by Europeans. When Europeans colonized much of Africa in the 1800s, Africans were sometimes used for forced labor. However, the practice of slavery was gradually outlawed. By 1930 slavery was illegal throughout Africa. Even today, however, Africans in some nations suffer under illegal slavery.

Africa After Slavery

Slave trading had drained Africa of generations of its population. Countless potential farmers, builders, craftsmen, and leaders were lost forever. In addition, the wars and raids set off by the slave trade weakened many African nations. A land that had produced great kingdoms and empires before the 1400s was not able to advance.

The Reality of "Freedom"

Slaves around the world were freed, but had few resources to start new lives. Many found themselves with no money or education. In the United States, many freed slaves had little choice but to continue working for their former masters.

Racism made life difficult for blacks everywhere. Even those with skills and education had trouble finding work. Many years passed before all black children were able to go to school.

Freed blacks everywhere had a long battle ahead of them. Freedom was good. But equal rights and fair treatment for all blacks would not come for a long time.

Many freed slaves had to continue living on plantations after they were emancipated.

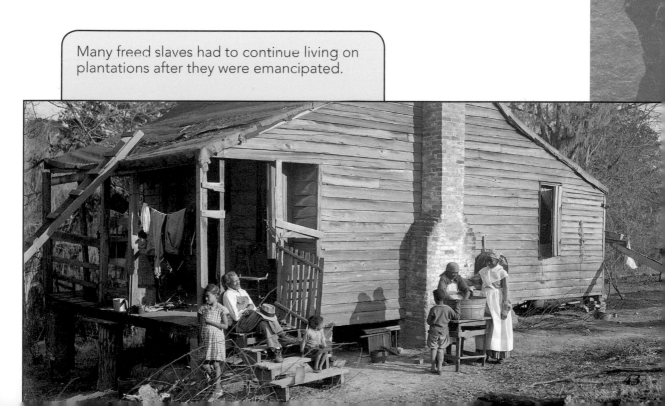

43

Timeline

1712	First slave rebellion occurs in New York City.
1739	First slave revolt occurs in the Southern United States—the Stono River Rebellion.
1772	British court frees escaped slave James Somerset.
1775	First American Anti-Slavery Society is founded by **Quakers** in Pennsylvania.
1787	British establish control in Sierra Leone as a place to resettle freed slaves.
1789	United States Constitution is signed; slavery remains legal.
1789	Freed slave Olaudah Equiano's autobiography is a big seller in Britain.
1793	Canada outlaws slavery.
1794–95	French Constitution of the Republic outlaws slavery.
1797	Slave army of Haiti under Toussaint Louverture wins freedom for all blacks. Louverture is governor from 1797 to 1802.
1800	Gabriel Prosser's slave army set to attack Richmond, Virginia. Prosser and his followers are arrested and hanged.
1802	Napoleon Bonaparte becomes French dictator, restoring slavery. Napoleon's army invades Haiti.
1804	Slave army of Haiti regroups and defeats French. Slavery is **abolished**.
1807	British Parliament makes it illegal to trade slaves.
1808	Atlantic slave trade is outlawed in United States.
1816	Barbados "Cane Fields" slave revolt is led by Bussa, an African slave.
1818	American Colonization Society is founded to return freed **African Americans** to Africa.

1818	Treaties among Britain, Spain, and Portugal end slave trade.
1818	France and Holland end slave trade.
1820–21	Land bought by United States in Liberia is set as homeland for freed slaves.
1822	Denmark Vesey enlists an army of slaves and free African Americans to take over Charleston, South Carolina. Vesey and the leaders are captured.
1829	Mexico abolishes slavery.
1831	Nat Turner kills 55 whites as his slave army rebels in Virginia.
1831	Jamaica's Sam Sharpe Rebellion and slaves of Montego Bay revolt.
1834	Britain's Slavery Abolition Act outlaws slavery in most of the Empire.
1847	Liberia becomes an independent country.
1850	United States passes the Fugitive Slave Law.
1861–65	United States Civil War.
1862	Abraham Lincoln signs the **Emancipation Proclamation**.
1864	13th Amendment is passed. Slavery becomes illegal in the United States.
1868	14th Amendment is passed. All freed slaves become citizens.
1870	15th Amendment is passed. All males over the age of 21 have the right to vote. No man could be denied due to race or previous enslavement.
1886	Cuba outlaws slavery.
1888	Brazil outlaws slavery.

Glossary

abolish to get rid of, outlaw, or destroy an institution

African American a person of African descent living in America

arsenal place where weapons are stored

boll the sac that holds the blossom from a plant such as cotton

bound servant a person bound to work for another for a set time

cash crop a crop that is grown to make money

colony a distant territory under the control of another nation

discharge to set free or dismiss from service

distillery a place where alcohol is made

emancipate to free someone from enslavement

Emancipation Proclamation document signed by President Abraham Lincoln freeing the slaves in Confederate states during Civil War

field hand a male or female slave who worked in the fields of a plantation

house servant a male or female slave who worked directly for the master's family and household

hymn a song of praise

Indian summer unusually warm weather in late autumn or early winter

Mende a group of people native to West Africa

overseer a person hired by a slave owner to oversee all work done by field hands

passive resistance a form of protest that does not involve violence, such as refusing to work or cooperate

plantation large farm, usually in the South, often with slaves

Quaker a member of a sect of Christianity

racism mistaken belief that a person's skin color determines his or her worth as a human being

ration the amount of something a person is allowed to use

Scramble for Africa or Race for Africa, period of time when European nations claimed and colonized land in Africa

slave patrollers guards hired to prevent slaves from escaping

transatlantic slave trade the business of capturing slaves in Africa and selling them across the Atlantic to buyers in the Americas

Underground Railroad a network of volunteers throughout the United States that hid fugitive slaves and guided them northward to freedom

Find Out More

Books

Barr, Gray. *Slavery in the United States.* Chicago: Heinemann Library, 2004.

Donlan, Leni. *Following Freedom: The Underground Railroad.* Chicago: Raintree, 2007.

Hall, Margaret C. *The History and Activities of the Civil War.* Chicago: Heinemann Library, 2006.

Meadows, James. *Slavery: The Struggle for Freedom.* Mankato, Minn.: Child's World, 2009.

Rossi, Ann. *Freedom Struggle: The Anti-Slavery Movement 1830-1865.* Washington, D.C.: National Geographic, 2005.

Websites

Africans in America: America's Journey Through Slavery
www.pbs.org/wgbh/aia

Encyclopedia Britannica's Guide to Black History
http://search.eb.com/blackhistory

The National Underground Railroad Freedom Center
http://www.freedomcenter.org/underground-railroad/

Slavery and Freedom in the Caribbean
http://www.nationalarchives.gov.uk/caribbeanhistory/slavery-negotiating-freedom.htm

Index